Raw Silk

Also by Meena Alexander

Poetry

Stone Roots

House of a Thousand Doors

River and Bridge

The Shock of Arrival: Reflections on Postcolonial Experience
    (poems and essays)

Illiterate Heart

Prose

Women in Romanticism: Mary Wollstonecraft,
    Dorothy Wordsworth, and Mary Shelley

Nampally Road

Manhattan Music

Fault Lines: A Memoir

Raw Silk

Meena Alexander

TriQuarterly Books
Northwestern University Press
Evanston, Illinois

TriQuarterly Books
Northwestern University Press
www.nupress.northwestern.edu

Printed in the United States of America

10 9 8 7 6 5 4 3

ISBN-13: 978-0-8101-5156-7 (cloth)
ISBN-10: 0-8101-5156-1 (cloth)
ISBN-13: 978-0-8101-5158-1 (paper)
ISBN-10: 0-8101-5158-8 (paper)

Library of Congress Cataloging-in-Publication data are available
from the Library of Congress.

♾ The paper used in this publication meets the minimum
requirements of the American National Standard for Information
Sciences – Permanence of Paper for Printed Library Materials,
ANSI Z39.48-1992.

FOR ADAM AND SVATI

The Sackcloth – hangs upon the nail –
The Frock I used to wear –
But where my moment of Brocade –
My – drop – of India?

– *Emily Dickinson*

Contents

—

—

Raw Silk

Dialogue by a City Wall

HE: I need to smell you.
Come near the window, the city hovers there.

I want to be sure you're not a girl made of clouds
with only a wound for a mouth.

SHE: You gave me a book,
you touched the red ink.

You said: Look, that's my name.
Why did you tremble when you gave me that book?

HE: I know you already and it's not from any place.
You're the woman whose scent has driven me mad,

I thumb through pages packed with syllables and cannot find you.
Tell me your name, come let me write you.

SHE: The instruments of war
are buried underwater.

Incense wafts from the curtained rooms,
a tall tree makes a fountain.

5

On the leaves of the tree
outside your wall it is written:

I am Sita and Iphigenia, Demeter and Draupadi.
I am not fit for burning.

Ancestors

They are bicycling into the sun.
He has a dhoti on under his coat
and a briefcase with LYRIC
marked in big letters.

She has a sari in lime green
and socks and a backpack
that is filled with scraps
of torn silk.

She drops a fan as she
races past the balustrade
into sky blue water.
The fan opens

and slips into the shape
an oyster makes when
it whorls a pearl.
Something of great price

is torn from her and the man
on his bicycle who is wheeling
at the edge of the crater
cannot see or hear.

Soon as the poet had it
they will be pecked to death
by a partridge. Soon they will drop
into dark water.

1. Aftermath

There is an uncommon light in the sky
Pale petals are scored into stone.

I want to write of the linden tree
That stoops at the edge of the river

But its leaves are filled with insects
With wings the color of dry blood.

At the far side of the river Hudson
By the southern tip of our island

A mountain soars, a torrent of sentences
Syllables of flame stitch the rubble

An eye, a lip, a cut hand blooms
Sweet and bitter smoke stains the sky.

2. Invisible City

Sweet and bitter smoke stains the air
The verb *stains* has a thread torn out

I step out to the linden grove
Bruised trees are the color of sand.

Something uncoils and blows at my feet.
Sliver of mist? Bolt of beatitude?

A scrap of what was once called sky?
I murmur words that come to me

Tall towers, twin towers I used to see
A bloody seam of sense drops free.

By Liberty Street, on a knot of rubble
In altered light, I see a bird cry.

3. Pitfire

In altered light I hear a bird cry.
By the pit, tor of metal, strut of death.

Birdsong yet. *Liturgie de cristal.*
Flesh in fiery pieces, mute sediments of love.

Shall a soul visit her mutilated parts?
How much shall a body be home?

Under these burnt balconies of air
Autumnal duty that greets us.

At night, a clarinet solo I put on:
Birdsong pitched to a gorge, a net of cries.

In the news, a voice caught on a lost line:
"We've even struck the bird's throat."

Hard Rowing

Take my arm right
where it was blown off
and set it in your sleeve.

Silk will not
sear flesh
as cotton does.

Can you smell sweat
from stones and raw bones
flowering?

Each thing
grows tiny in packing,
even souls.

Two or more hand
in hand leapt off
the tightrope of ash.

Do you see
the sash of blood
where the shops were?

What a circus with Frantz
and Mohandas
squabbling onshore.

What was burst seals,
even the torn
host of names.

Fallen here
let's row hard with
our precarious oars.

Kabir Sings in a City
of Burning Towers

What a shame
they scared you so
you plucked your sari off,
crushed it into a ball,

then spread it
on the toilet floor.
Sparks from the towers
fled through the weave of silk.

With your black hair
and sun dark skin
you're just a child of earth.
Kabir the weaver sings:

O men and dogs
in times of grief
our rolling earth
grows small.

Ghalib's Ghost

When I was young mother called me chick chick chick.
Father read *Conference of the Birds* aloud to me.

I was partridge, the one with speckled wings
poking here and there with her beak, gobbling stones.

One afternoon, the roof blew off our house.
Roofs blew off many houses, courtyards filled with clouds.

I fell from our upper room into a circus.
Petals paraded through hot skies, veiling sun and moon.

Paintings had eyes, lips, thighs torn out.
Bullets swam in grandmother's well.

I had to take my glasses off for that sack I was forced
to pull over my head. Peering out as best I could

I saw leopards curled in heat
and Ghalib's ghost hidden in a burka, pouncing at crickets.

School Yard

You live in a place called Providence
but you grew up in this city
by these walls,
played stickball by the river,
leapt over a path into the playground
by Battery Park.
Now the walls are on fire.
When you call I tell you the fields
by the river are sprinkled with ash.
The children have fled
the new school yard
where they carry the wounded in,
men and women half alive,
skin smoldering.

For my son, Adam Kuruvilla

September Sunlight

A woman in army castoffs
goes down the steps to the river.
A dove flutters each shoulder bone.
Here Seiji, here Setsuko, she murmurs.
Stay brother sun, stay sister moon.
Not so long ago in Hiroshima
woman in kimono, bird, and cloud
turned to shadows staining the ground.
Through branches of the sun
I watch her go down the steps to the river.
Her shadow brushes the lilac tree.
The birds are naked as birds well might be,
they sing to no one in particular.

For Shuntaro Tanikawa

1. Color of Home

I met you by Battery Park where the bridge once was.
Invisible it ran between the towers.
What made you follow me, O ghost in black cutaways?

Dear Mr. Lorca I address you,
filled with a formal feeling.
You were tongue tied on the subway till a voice cried out:

Thirty-fourth Street, last stop on the D.
It's the Empire State, our tallest again,
time to gather personal belongings, figure out redemption.

You leaned into my ribs muttering:
Did you hear that, you seller of salt
and gatherer of ash just as your foremothers were?

How the world goes on and on.
Have you ever seen a bullfight?
What do you have strapped to your back?

Then quieter, under your breath:
Let's survive the last stop together.
I knew a Hindu ballerina once,

nothing like you, a quick, delicate thing.
I walked with her by the river
those months when English fled from me

and the young men of Manhattan
broke cherry twigs and scribbled on my skin
till one cried out – I am the boy killed by dark water,

surely you know me?
Then bolt upright you whispered:
Why stay on this island?

See how it's ringed by water and flame?
You who have never seen Granada –
tell me, what is the color of home?

2. Casida of a Flowering Tree

Go to Monticello, tell me who's buried
under the flowering cherry tree.
Is it Jefferson's daughter with honey–colored hair?
Or Jefferson's son who served his father
burst figs on a blue–veined plate,
then crept into the old man's room
to stroke a coverlet seamed with silk?
Glass ornaments from Paris hurt his fist.
The house threaded with weights started to float.
The young man wept till his tears
flowered in Córdoba.
I have written about him in the song
you read as a child. The one with the line
at five in the afternoon. Don't you recall?

3. Central Park, Carousel

June already, it's your birth month,
nine months since the towers fell.
I set olive twigs in my hair
torn from a tree in Central Park.
I ride a painted horse, its mane a sullen wonder.
You are behind me on a lilting mare.
You whisper – What of happiness?
Dukham, Federico. Smoke fills my eyes.
Young, I was raised to a sorrow song
short fires and stubble on a monsoon coast.
The leaves in your cap are very green.
The eyes of your mare never close.
Somewhere you wrote: *Despedida*,
if I die leave the balcony open!

Hungriest Heart

Hungriest heart where are you now?
Wrapped in blue with starched white blouse,

hair tucked into braids so tight
sparrows sought you out.

All your girl's equipage, sac of eggs,
pouch of blood, knotted into skin.

You are fleeing what was meant to be real:
a house without wheels

the bone's high arc
without let or forgiveness.

Why call it home –
O cuckoo's cradle!

For a Friend Whose Father Was Killed on the Lahore Border in the 1965 War between India and Pakistan

I come to you nothing in my arms,
just this bundle.

Cloth covering what the pity of war
could not render up – the bones of a father.

The horses of Uttarakhand wept salt,
their necks were torqued.

Birds stalk clouds, clouds hang cold,
on a hill of gold, stick insects clamor.

Where are the burnt plains of the Punjab?
The killing fields of Partition?

At the mouth of Central Park
apple blossom sifts your breath

and you search for me.
I long to come running to you, hair flying,

a girl again in the moist air,
in the ordinary light of a garden.

But how shall I hold you,
this bundle in my arms – love's fierce portion?

How shall we face the torn rim of green,
the horses of Columbus cut in steel?

Firefly

I stand here my two hands out,
there is smoke in the trees.

In Naroda Patiya, in Godhra,
children sing in the ground.

I have crawled in and out of the sky.
Who am I?

My brother is a field of hurt wheat,
my father a singing ruin.

Mud in her mouth
my mother cries in me.

Something is scrawled on doors
I cannot see.

A firefly threads my eye.
Who am I?

Child, Stone, Sea

A child comes from the sea
there is a stone in his hand.

He says "Here is your jawbone,"
I take it from him.

In Gugu Dlamini Park
under green leaves of the fever tree

I sit on a bench marked WHITES ONLY.
A bird with no beak is singing to me.

A child comes from the sea
there is a stone in his hand.

He says "Here is your grandfather's thighbone,"
he sets it on my knee.

The sea has many sleeves
one is fire, one is silk, one is torn cotton.

Keep me from harm
I cry to the child

he shakes his head.
He turns away from me.

Under his ribs is a golden saxophone
the color of the sun

when torn leaves
burst through air.

—

On the Bay of Plenty pier
I pass a man let loose from a prison cell.

The sun's throat is torn cotton,
he whispers to me,

the moon's cheek is burnt silk.
Your mother's mother was a satyagrahi,

she knew the uses of fire.
I see that his skin is filled with monsoon clouds.

There is salt in his beard.
He carries the child on his back.

At night, hearing him sing,
I loosen my sari.

I walk through the walls
of my room into the sea.

Green Parasol

Sweet blossom of hair and flesh
fourteen years ago you tore me up so swift.

They set you blue, bawling to my left breast.
Later I fit you hungry still

between elbow and wrist,
dreamt us rib to rib

in the chiseled ivory box
your great–grandmother

bore north over red hills
as part of her wedding dowry.

⁓

In the studio on Sixty–first I watch your torque
of groin and thigh, a dancer's labor

toes strung to the polished floor,
knees flounced in precise pirouette.

Later you hunch in your room
scrawling hot alphabets

in the margins of
Their Eyes Were Watching God.

Homework done
you're Instant Messaging your friends

chat of the latest rap
or boyband or bandanna.

—

You're quiet now.
Here take this gift,

strip off the worn silk,
tear the cloudy tissue paper.

It's all I have
this moist quilt work

of rooms and balconies,
continents torn,

tampered with,
bloodthirsty.

—

My love, my little phoenix,
your mother the old nest is quite undone.

Soar over the Bronx River,
set fire to old straw,

light up the broken avenues of desire.
Then be a girl like any other,

in soft mist, in flowering sunlight,
at the rim of stone gates,

raise a green parasol
under a green tree.

For my daughter, Svati Mariam

Raw Silk

I

Open the door or I'll faint hearing amma's voice –
Where is the silk from your grandmother's sari?

Raw silk
brought all the way from Varanasi.

In another life I crouched on the stone floor reading poetry
Le ciel est, par-dessus le toit . . .

cette paisible rumeur-là, that sort of thing
and the town was literally blazing:

guns, grenades, blisters of smoke
on marketplace and mosque.

Through the bars of a whitewashed schoolroom
Verlaine peering, above his head a palm tree cradling the sun.

Far from Kerala amma fed me tales.
After her wedding, years after the Salt March,

grandmother coaxed mulberries
from monsoon soil, clouds ran riot,

silkworms coiled under the skin of leaves,
berries dripped free,

the courtyard was a sea of blood.
When grandmother died

the wedding sari with its brocade
saved from the bonfire Gandhi had ordained

was wrapped in muslin
set in a wardrobe, the door locked tight.

     II

Child, it's bad enough to be in a desert land
why mutter poems in a language I can't understand?

How could I say that in the sandstorm
I heard Verlaine singing,

Rimbaud setting fire to a felucca.
By the Mahdi's palace

syllables run amok,
Gordon's head nodding on a stake

as red dates clustered
on the bough of immortality,

hence poems I committed to memory,
flute music guiding me through the vertigo of history.

I wept in sorrow I could scarcely bear
for a mother killed on the street,

a girl child pinned to a bed
as ancient hands cut at her

and smoke rose from an island in the Nile
where bricks were baked for insurrection.

Should I cast it all away
be the girl who can't remember?

Could I have uttered what I didn't know –
when silk comes out of the silkworm's hole

it is the color of colostrum.
It was Khartoum and it was not.

O inwardness its own reward
as the sun rises on the city of God.

III

Amma there are silkworms
dancing in the firmament

above your head and mine,
and the mother of worms

doffs her veil
and darkens her lips

and sets a crown
of mulberry leaves on my head.

When I open the drawer
to search for silk

I touch smoke,
raw silk turned to smoke in the night's throat.

Rumors for an Immigrant

I. FIFTH AVENUE PLAZA

Water slips down a concrete wall.
In the plaza, she touches a metal table, a chair, a notebook.

Noon already, each thing swallows its own shadow
murmuring, I cannot flee you.

She loosens her hair, becomes a woman in a silk sari
on a high balcony, the trellis cut in bone.

Rumors clip the air, spread their wings
and swarm through the plaza.

Suddenly she feels hot.
Draws her hair back, a comb glistens in her hand,

she pulls out a pocket mirror, puckers her lips,
she tries to make small-scale order

(two black eyes, dark skin, two nostrils,
that sort of thing) out of bristling confusion.

From mouth to shining mouth news darts.
In fields by the river indigo burns.

Gandhi enters Central Park, smoke in his palms.
He raises a charka, a dove coos, fluttering out of his dhoti.

Behind him, pots and pans lashed to bicycle rickshaws,
come the people.

There is no homeland anymore,
all nations are abolished, a young man cries.

In the lake rumors flicker, make luminous habitation.
Allen Ginsberg leaps from the reeds

holding hands with a young man from Conakry,
dead already, turned into a star,

shot forty–one times by police as he stood in his own doorway.
Gently loiter, he sings.

On his charka Gandhi strums a tune:
I stop somewhere, waiting for you.

She has heard the rumor no one will have a homeland.
She opens up her notebook,

she wants to flee her past,
she thinks she can live on the white page.

Wo ist Heimat?
She murmurs this in a tongue she does not understand.

Wen Beitak? Naad evida?
Sitting very straight she writes in her best hand:

I have floated on the river Spree.
Seen Brecht's Theater from the outside in,

tucked my body into two suitcases,
with a hole cut between,

hung in a museum at Checkpoint Charlie.
Tired suddenly she stops writing, rubs her wrist.

Three months ago she met a man with a hurt wrist.
He used to live not far from Mohenjo Daro.

In her notebook she speaks to him:
I come from where Marco Polo turned,

as for Mohenjo Daro, it is covered in dirt.
The invisible cities burn in me.

Here come under my ribs.
She claps her hand to her lips

lest the wind turn this into a rumor
that reaches Gandhi's ears.

She whispers the immigrant's name,
adds, in her mother tongue, *Ende priyen!*

She feels all her days and nights are etched
on his lonely skin

in script so exquisite and spare
no one has deciphered it.

In time she will be to him as the air he breathes
so he forgets her utterly,

yet his mouth will be tucked to her ear,
marking a wild rose, her raw lips to his wrist.

Blue Lotus

It is not enough to cover the rock with leaves
— *Wallace Stevens*

I

Twilight, I stroll through stubble fields
clouds lift, the hope of a mountain.
What was distinct turns to mist,

what was fitful burns the heart.
When I dream of my tribe gathering
by the red soil of the Pamba River

I feel my writing hand split at the wrist.
Dark tribute or punishment, who can tell?
You kiss the stump and where the wrist

bone was, you set the stalk of a lotus.
There is a blue lotus in my grandmother's garden,
its petals whirl in moonlight like this mountain.

II

An altar, a stone cracked down the spine,
a shelter, a hovel of straw and sperm
out of which rise a man and a woman

and one is a ghost though I cannot tell which
for the sharpness between them scents
even the orchids, a sharing of things

invisible till the mountain fetches
itself out of water out of ice out of sand
and they each take tiny morsels

of the mountain and set it on banana leaves
and as if it were a feast of saints
they cry out to their dead and are satisfied.

III

I have climbed the mountain and cleared
away the sand and ice using first my bare hands
then a small knife. Underneath I found

the sign of the four-cornered world, *gammadion,*
which stands for migration, for the scattering
of the people. The desolation of the mothers

singing in their rock houses becomes us,
so too the child at the cliff's edge
catching a cloud in her palm

as stocks of blood are gathered on the plain,
spread into sheaves, a circlet for bones
and flint burns and the mountain resurrects itself.

IV

Tribe, tribute, tribulation:
to purify the tongue and its broken skin
I am learning the language again,

a new speech for a new tribe.
How did I reach this nervous empire,
sharp store of sense?

Donner un sens plus pur etc. etc.
does not work so well anymore,
nor *calme bloc ici-bas.*

Blunt metals blossom.
Children barter small arms.
Ground rules are abolished.

The earth has no capitals.
In my distinct notebooks
I write things of this sort.

Monsoon clouds from the shore
near my grandmother's house
float through my lines.

I take comfort in sentences.
"Who cares what you write?"
someone cries.

A hoarse voice, I cannot see the face.
He smells like a household ghost.
There can be no concord between us.

I search out a bald rock between two trees,
ash trees on the riverbank
on an island city where towers blazed.

This is my short
incantation,
my long way home.

William, Rabindranath, Czeslaw,
Mirabai, Anna, Adrienne
reach out your hands to me.

Now stones have tongues.
Sibilant scattering,
stormy grace!

Petroglyph

Girl grown woman   fire   mother of fire
— *Muriel Rukeyser*

I

Darting lines of a petroglyph at Stornorrfors up north
by the river's rim, an elk with a lifeline through it,
to the right a human, arms stuck out, feet too,
a dancing thing sworn to four points of the compass.
A light wind strikes up,
drizzling grass seeds over a pile of ash,
our feet bound in leather knotted with floating strings.
Dear, I have nothing invested in narrative,
not in any way that should make you nervous.
The earth our green and fragrant home.
Yes, *home* we like to say mindful of what has brutalized
our soil and hurt the sheen of wind and rain.
And to argue as some do that fear incites
the sublime gets us precisely nowhere.

II

Remember the sage of Königsberg? Thirty–three,
burnt out already, pacing the stairwell, in top hat and spats,
figuring out footnotes to a doctoral dissertation on Fire.
Sparks fly from his wrist and from the throat
of a woman first glimpsed in a water meadow.
Who can tell what the brilliant Immanuel
can or can't have had in mind?
In his *Physische Geographie* volcanoes blow their spouts off,
wild beasts clamber up higgledy–piggledy ruins.
On the ground, the thingness
of forms battened down as far as thought might latch
onto the tiniest button, tender bell of flesh.
Desire strapped lest it stray
into a mismatched nature, promiscuous geography.

White men being the flower of perfection, all others drop away.
Burmese women dress in slovenly fashion;
Hottentots smell; Indians ruin everything with their oily skin.
Grass though needful for the ox, also for man's subsistence,
cannot help us reckon why beings need to exist.
Why this taxonomy riveted by skin color?
Why strip some persons raw? Might we think space
through skin, muscle, and bone as bright vitality?
Questions startle each other, hook, and point to desire.
See, there's Kant by a stairwell in an inner room
he paces, thought tormented, then stoops to listen hard.
Petals splatter from the plum branch by the river,
also fragments of a cheekbone, an earlobe dangling a pearl.
A hot, discordant music wells up from earth's core.

➤

III

After the glyphs cut in granite, after the broken sky
we returned to the hotel by the river Umeälv.
I drew back curtains and stared at black water.
A house was afloat on that river, bright the moon,
and in the bright house a child, her face covered
with a hat of wool so red, darkness fled from it.
I thought it you, brought back in time's mercy
a breathing power, the present flashing.
In sleep I saw myself a five-year child
her house afloat and in her house a man
his flesh in tints no chords can stake.
Blunt, caustic red. What instrument of rage
can the wind fling? I hate your knucklebone!
the child cries. She sees Kant on his bookshelf.

—

IV

When I was a child I saw the sea burn.
I need to tell you this. How often
I have written that line, no page to put it on,
no voice to mark it mine. On the Indian Ocean
I turned five, aboard a white steamer.
I left a house behind: red stone in the room
where the man stood, flesh marking a staircase.
Rib cage, a furious flower that cracks space.
Now I live on an island by the mid-Atlantic shore.
Home is where when I go, they let me in.
I sit by a window that gives onto a river.
I write at a small metal desk with rolling wheels.
Sometimes the floor tilts and clouds the color of salt
make me giddy, as if I were a girl again.

I stare in the mirror and see a woman
I seem to recognize. Her hair a morning ruin she sings:
Consider these burnt balconies of air!
Whether we are in Asia or in a northern land
where the sun holes down at noon so darkness
frets our joints, we will speak to each other.
Our language pierced by gunfire, precise as it can get,
alphabets stripped to skin and ligament.
On lower Broadway under the hood of stone,
tall towers cherish bits of flaming bone.
Uptown where sky meets river, barges drift.
They bear jags of twisted metal, urns of priceless ash.
Who are we now?
What is this heavy water rushing to the sea?

—

V

Once setting up your paintings in Buenos Aires
you shut the window tight, covered it in cloth to turn
the room entire into a white cube. You did not want to hear
young couples making picnic on the wild grass,
nor children striking fists against plastic balls,
nor the older ones sniffing glue.
You set your paintings up each echoing the other,
the whole entitled *Riposte*. Where the face went down
side up the room filled with invisible flames
that Kant had dreamt of. Later you said
"To fill a room with space is a transaction
I understand." Now your hand with the brush upright
scans space. You are searching for me.
In the very element that severs us.

—

VI

By a rock in Europe's frozen north
we saw elk rear into the bitter blood of the sun.
We touched leftovers from a fire, a mound of ashes,
a man's coat, sleeves torn and muddied.
Or did it belong to a woman unhoused,
poverty's use, the horizon of care affixed to true north?
Turning from the river you pointed out a figure
scratched between twin elk, a face for hunger,
a female glyph, wide open on black rock.
Our clothes are prized off in a brutal wind
and these poems, cloud–tossed particulars,
sharp with need, sprung in the ash of my new country.
Searchlights twist where a glass garden hung,
iron cranes cluster, stanzas drop their skirts and flee.

—

VII

What war is this? On our island city
we cannot round its edges, pulse its scope.
The scent of flesh and charred wires infects our speech.
Riding the metal subways, underground passages
wired for speed, I read a poet who grew up here:
Towers falling   a dream of towers.   Necessity of fountains.
I stand by a burning pit, a burial ground for thousands,
souls loosed from their bodies, swirling.
I hear names for ancient places: Istalif, Kabul, Kandahar.
I see women shrug off their veils, let sunlight
strike their cheeks. Women casting burkas
into flames no water can check. Children poking bits
of metal in unplowed land, a necklace of sorrow
mothers bear, throats parched with blood.

Yesterday I stood on the street where I used to live.
I watched a cathedral in flames.
Fire razed the wooden rafters of the northern wall
and struck the chalice in Abraham's hand.
I saw votive candles, dewdrops burst in heat.
I was near the door I had carried my infant through,
wrapped in a blanket the color of summer leaves,
her skull bones so frail fingers of air could have poked through.
We are knit in secret. We bear the thumbprint of mystery.
I write to you in dreams. After birth where do we go?
Hidden on an island by the Baltic coast
where the wind whispers cold psalms of praise
you start a new self–portrait. *Woman with Petroglyph,*
or Self as Two Tall Women by the Sea.

VIII

I try to imagine what she understood
crouched at earth's ledge, the maker of petroglyphs,
her rough and ready skins blown about her,
hand with adze held out, reckoning an ancient shelter,
this earth our green, imperiled home.
I try to imagine the philosopher on his deathbed,
dreaming of fire that alters all substances
known to geography. Grass rock skin bits of bone
become in and of themselves ornaments of unity.
Immaterial insignia. So what sears the mind to order
need not subtract from the manifold of space,
cast love awry. Elsewhere in a meadow of hot bones,
grown girls make implacable plans
then rise on tiptoe with lost larks to sing.

Porta Santa

You bought rolls of bread so hot
they might have been stones from my childhood.

I followed you, twisted my ankle,
fainted an instant, losing body.

Then someone whose hair glows in the dark
led me to a grove of olive trees.

I turned back to the Arno
I saw the blue Giotto saw,

I wept at stones
that stored so much light.

＿

So where are you now?
In the transparent phone booth in Fiumicino airport.

In the crush of those forced to draw metal carts
piled with open cartons, precious scraps of clothing.

On the runway beside darkened palms
jets hover, wings spilling sparks.

And the door you led me through?
Porta Santa

beside the room where I could not sleep
beside the street named for the serpents

beside the blind beggar covered in sackcloth
– *Vieni, vieni qui!* –

terrible guide
what would Dante have made of you?

Door of water, door of earth,
mirror of gold

I stepped through,
hearing the voices of pilgrims cry:

Who will melt swords down,
fill courtyards with grain?

My soul naked, unashamed,
watching from a distance,

the body, old sari
washed with blue soap,

folded with care, set on a stone
Giotto painted beside a laughing shepherd boy.

Roman Ground

By the Roman Forum, speckled wildflowers,
olive trees roped by wind, fragments of granite before the flood.

In high school we used to leap over the barrier
till one night I saw a man – you pointed to a high window

in a building of the Campidoglio – threatening to leap.
See me? he cried as the police scurried around with blankets.

Who was he? A government clerk? A bus driver?
A silhouette stuck at a window ledge.

He cured me from jumping into the Temple of Saturn.
It was built by the Romans in a season of distress.

They had plagues, fires, famines, floods,
the ordinary rutted down, the sacred raised, florets of stone into
     the sun.

     ⟞

In your country you have floods, don't you?
I shut my eyes, saw stacks of rosewood floating in the courtyard,

stick thin shacks swirling in red water –
Pathiravil, athi pathie!

My father's father, lips bruised with betel,
each midnight crying himself home.

The house of God, walls tilted
under skies where the river of heaven pours.

—

A silence rose between us.
Cicadas bristled in the olive leaves, pigeons clustered on warm stone.

Lua, Lua Saturni I heard you murmur:
to loosen, grow lustrous, liberate.

I longed to touch your lips, nostrils, eyes.
Sharp and hard that need forcing me to front

the cornices of ruin, a sky creased with pink,
a ledge where a man stood crying

– Look, look at me! –
for one had ever seen him in his life before.

—

We stood on the littered earth
struck by sun into wheels of flame.

When I turned to you, your hair was smoldering,
there were tears in your eyes.

The wind was chill and I moved a little closer.
Then the stones beneath

and the stones around
grew steady in raw Roman ground.

Lago di Como

I search for a stone to sit on,
so I can look down into a valley and write lines
about a house I enter to find you.

I try to keep walking but after the storm
branches flood the path,
make me squint and crouch.

What I cannot peer through is memory:
a girl in a rosebush
thighs stuck with petals, scratch marks scarcely visible.

What floats into view
is a door I cannot go through.
But I want to go on and on until I reach you.

At the threshold of the house
I imagine fishhooks tethered to sunlight,
an old shirt hanging on a line.

It is after your bath,
your hair is wet and you are in front
of an oval mirror, rimmed in silver.

You are combing your hair.
Oh for an afternoon, eyes wide open,
filled with the moisture of love.

Door

By your door a sweet olive tree
a hole in its trunk:
swarm of bees in the lap of heaven!

Opening the Shutters

The faux windows are delectable.
They were painted with a fine brush
onto seventeenth–century stucco.

A maid in a striped blue dress
is hauling the shutters open
one by one in a serenade so still

I barely hear it.
She props up the shutters,
each on its metal pole,

smooths down her dress,
pleats well below the knees,
ardent stripes on a pale blue field.

I watch her from the crystalline
shadow of two trees,
Osmanthus fragrans, or sweet olive,

and *Euonymus europaeus,*
also known as *fortuni,* tree of good fortune.
In my grandmother's garden

there were other sorts of tree,
whose fragrance first forgotten
returns in dream to the sound

of a hand at a shutter's rim,
or tapping a palmyra fan
at the brink of a lagoon.

So to accumulate in noonday heat,
through the commonest turning,
chords of music

even in excessive sunlight
which is what this northern hilltop
brings in late summer

the hours, diaphanous, winged,
laden with heat, churning
time past and to come,

the burning heart not to be cast aside
and what we recognize as suffering
at its own unspeakable pitch

inching ever closer.
Through open shutters
we glimpse familiar figures

a man and woman and child
their faces cupped in mist.
How can I know

that in someone else's kitchen
she will take a knife
first to the child, then to herself?

I cannot bear what she has done,
I stare at the open shutters
weeping as the maid

with a luminous flourish
and for reasons entirely her own,
casts open the long door to the villa,

a corridor ringed with light,
at its very end
a Chinese jar still turning.

On its surface centuries ago
an unknown hand painted
a woman in a long robe,

gold hemmed with alizarin,
behind her another woman
and another,

the very last
holding a boy by the hand,
leading him into darkness.

Field in Summer

I had a simple childhood,
a mother and father to take care of me,
no war at my doorstep.

Stones sang
canticles in my mouth
as darkness rose.

Love, love where are they gone?
Father, mother, ink dark stars,
singing stones.

Triptych in a Time of War

Why hunch at the screen chipping syllables, chewing up rhyme?
You're no Forugh Farrokhzad, registered 678 in the sun's throat –
counting out jewels in the city street, dead in a car crash, aged
      thirty-two.

You're older by far, thrice failed your driving test,
never visited a leprosarium or Zahir al-Doleh cemetery in Tehran
where trees leak snow.

Where she whispers as a child might, smoking burnt-out tips,
a slip of a thing dressed in white rags
filled with light –

I did it, I got myself registered,
dressed myself up in an ID with a name.
So long 678 . . . O rattling law!

O the bomb is fear's flower
there is no love in the bomb,
only chaos the sea must swallow.

The flowers of Mesopotamia are tiny, blue edged,
driven under the skin of earth. But where can children hide?
The mouth of the cave is rimmed with red.

Spring brings the golden mustard seed and clouds of war
float over the ziggurat of Ur.
Enheduanna is poised on an alabaster disk.

She has nose breasts hands a poet needs, also
that sweet etcetera, dark flower who sheds blood and eggs and
        praises
to be sung at twilight into the high hold of heaven.

You remember her and Forugh too who fought against pain.
Their stanzas flicker on the Internet,
you flee a windowless office,

climb the stairs to the eighth floor, enter a high room.
Light spills through sloping glass,
clouds drift and float,

you hear the clatter of knives in the cafeteria.
On an eastern wall the Dove of Tanna,
wings raised, mute blessing in a time of need.

The artist born a year after Forugh cut up aluminum for the dove's
        tail,
infolding fire, icon of earth struck free of floodwaters,
pediment of peace beneath the arrow's flight.

You have come to a high room
in search of language that could tell of love,
of love alone, uncumbered and to search for it, as for justice

even in the guise of what has no words and cannot speak
and must lie down in the dark
hungry and unappeased.

—

III

Out of the spotted beak of the dove,
out of the olive tree axed into bits,
out of blood a child touches to her lips murmuring words no one
    else can hear,

out of the eyes of the woman who stands shock still in sunlight
and flings open the door
and Bombay rushes in a tiger that brings her to her knees:

a vividness of island sky and wind
(she strolls by a slurry wall that held back island waters after
    catastrophe),
visionary company, electric water, fiery wind

where what is torn and severed slips out of soiled skin,
is seized in simple nakedness,
named and healed.

So turning to little bits of wisdom – do not hurt, do not cut,
love in all the right places and the wrong.
There is no fault in love.

The boughs know this cracking free of winter
in the cemetery where Forugh's body lies,
so too the Dove of Tanna.

It takes flight from the eastern wall of 365 Fifth Avenue
and settles on the ziggurat of Ur,
by a crater where a bomb burst.

Returning to the office without walls
you hear Enheduanna cry
O the ziggurat of Ur is crowned with doves!

You hear her words unfurl on the screen,
bare sound, filled with longing,
syllables of raw silk, this poem.

Red Bird

A red bird shoots
through a cloud of leaves,
the sky is filled with sparks,
I sit eating water chestnuts.
*These are the best
years of your life.*
Whose voice is that?
The nuts are pale
as running milk,
their lids, bruised green.
A boy with brown eyes
wields a knife, sets it all
at my knee. *Madam
these paniphal
are for you. Eat please.*
I sit in the light
of a boy's eyes,
chewing water chestnuts.
The shed where they raped
the women is far away.
Far away the flung bones
piled in the shape
of a cross.
This is my country.
I was born by the Ganga
close by as a bird flies.

Amrita

I was dressed
in a fine muslin
sari over which
I wore a fur coat.

Behind me an old
man with camera.
Picture perfect
nothing
cast a shadow.

II

My father
Umrao Singh
fasted for
fifteen days
took a photo
of his self
in skimpy
loincloth.
Waist delicate
as a heron's neck.

Later my nephew
played with light,
set us edge
to edge.
In time's transparency
father and I
shone bright.

III

Nights I get no rest.
A rubber ball
bounces off
Parisian tapestries,
lands in my fur coat
splashes me.

Hold me
hold me a child cries.
My name is
Yunus.
Yunus can you hear me?

He stands there
half naked,
his green shirt
torn, flapping.
His belly and ribs
smoking.

He skips away.
I see his bottom
burst like a raw fruit
with the flames
they tossed him in.

I put out my arms
to touch him
but father's
tripod
trips me up.

IV

I want to whisper
I am Amrita
sweet
as burnt gold
in the *dargah*
of Wali Gujarati.

Here are my paints,
my brushes
bright as bone.
Come to me.

In Naroda Patiya

Dark eyes
the color of burnt
almonds, face
slashed, lower
down where her belly
shone
a wet gash.
Three armed men.
Out they plucked
a tiny heart
beating with her own.
No cries
were heard
in the city.
Even the sparrows
by the temple gate
swallowed their song.

Searching for a Tomb
over Which They Paved a Road

Where is the tomb
of Wali Gujarati?
Gold leaf scatters
in the wind.
His poems cry out for feet
hands throat
for genitals and mouth.
Surat has forgotten him.
He sang her praises
to the moon.
And now?
Where is my skin
my bones?
I am the poet of a city
in ruins
burnt by the sun
bound to the moon.
The reeds
by the river
are lashed to swords.
My dust is in the mouth
of the bloodied rose.

1. Lyric with Doves

I set doves on
my writing fingers
feel them fly.
The page is hushed.
From way beyond
hyenas howl.
There is too much
riveted into death.
What they bruised
and broke
– thighs arms
lips throat
precious inner organs –
is brushed
with brilliant ink,
cavalcades of pain.
It rains in your city,
the heart's
flung back.
Torn bodies
clattering
in an ox–drawn cart.

2. Slow Dancing

Dear Mr. Gandhi
please say something
about the carnage in your home state.

How did you feel when they shut
the gates of Sabarmati Ashram
that February night

and the wounded clung outside?
What has happened to ahimsa?
Is it just for the birds and the bees?

What lips, what soles
swarmed across the river?
Is it hot on the other side?

Oh, so many questions, sir,
I cannot help myself
I cannot shut my mouth.

It's hard to hear you,
birds peck at sounds,
maggots gnaw since

even syllables have skin.
The kingdom of heaven
is tiny as a mustard seed

and you have crawled therein.
Mist pours from mango trees,
the moon soars in a sea of blood.

I see you at the rim of heaven
grown older still, bewildered, stooped,
dhoti flecked with drops of mud,

face seared by a moon
that has nothing
except its own inhuman glow,

the archipelago of light
afloat in monsoon air
where souls frail as pinpricks go.

Dear Mr. Gandhi
please talk to me now.
I am slow dancing

in the dark
with the untimely dead
and that is all I know.

3. Bengali Market

Dear Mr. Gandhi
It was cold the day the masjid
was torn down stone by stone,
colder still at the heart of Delhi.

Ten years later entering Bengali market
I saw a street filled with bicycles,
girls with rushing hair, boys in bright caps.
I heard a voice cry

Can you describe this?
It sounded like a voice
from a city crusted with snow
to the far north of the Asian continent.

I saw him then, your grandson,
in a rusty three-wheeler
wrapped up in what wools he could muster.
Behind him in red letters

a sign: DR. GANDHI'S CLINIC.
So he said, embracing me, You've come back.
Then pointing to the clinic –
It's not that I'm sick

that gentleman gets my mail and I his.
That is why I am perched in this contraption.
I cannot stay long, it is Id–ul–Fitr.
I must greet friends in Old Delhi, wish them well.

Later he sought me out in dreams,
in a high kitchen in sharp sunlight
dressed in a khadi kurta, baggy jeans.
He touched my throat in greeting.

Listen, my sweet, for half of each year,
after the carriage was set on fire
after the Gujarat killings,
I disappear into darkness.

In our country there are two million dead
and more for whom no rites were said.
No land on earth can bear this.
Rivers are crisscrossed with blood.

All day I hear the scissor bird cry
cut cut cut cut cut.
It is the bird Kālidāsa heard
as he stood singing of buried love.

Now our boys and girls take
flight on rusty bicycles.
Will we be cured? I cried.
And he–We have no tryst with destiny.

My hands like yours are stained
with juice of the pomegranate.
Please don't ask for my address.
I am in and out of Bengali market.

4. Gandhi's Bicycle (My Muse Comes to Me)

I come to you with a jute bag
filled with bits of cloth
marked with the colors of heaven.

I have meditated long and hard on the poems
you read at the Akademi.
In "Ancestors" you have grandparents

male and female on wheels
cycling around ground zero.
Bipedality is no longer possible.

The earth is cut from underfoot.
Have you seen the photo
of Gandhi on his bicycle, in South Africa?

He tried to walk the earth
the British made fun of him,
also for the way he dressed.

Catastrophe drove you to
a grandmother in a sari on a bicycle
furiously pedaling where the towers

once stood, also a grandfather, I presume,
with briefcase marked LYRIC.
But don't lose sight of Epic.

That very month, that very day,
September 11 in 1893,
Swami Vivekananda stood in Chicago

a dark rose on its stalk.
Chicago is in the Midwest of course –
Sisters and brothers of America, he began,

and there was thunderous applause.
How many would dare say that now?
But we need to say that you and I

even in the teeth of war. Come closer now.
Do you hear the still sad music
of children killed in Godhra and Naroda Patiya?

Come closer to this table, cut
from a tamarind tree in my grandfather's garden.
Each poet needs a table

to lay her wares out, don't you agree?
You can write your poems here
so they gather the sour sweet light of eternity.

One last thing, please don't
keep writing letters to Gandhiji.
He has gone through so much already.

Sometimes I dream he's hidden
in a cupboard with three doors
where he's also stashed his bicycle.

Fragile Places

The world is a forest on fire
— *Sankara*

Rain blazed over Tiruvella – the red gorge.
Sankara speak to me:

carry me through the house of silt,
the low–slung bone,

wind me in raw silk,
cry to the gulls on the seacoast.

Hulls, dhows, catamarans,
Persian panoplies, Portuguese men–of–war,

clusters of jellyfish in the sea's craw,
baptism of spray

the passage rough,
horizon scrawled with stars.

I lay with you at the water's edge
a red rose blossomed in my breast.

Nothing is changed
by the strength of reflection

and everything.
Raw silk in the torn cupboard

of the will. *Two annas for soap,*
three annas for a bundle of matches,

grandmother wrote, *four annas*
for a rag so she will not hurt her hands.

Later I will tie up my notes with string,
letters too, neatly knot them.

Grandmother polished her sandals
stepped into the long boat

that drew her to Kaladi,
your birthplace.

Her house I inherit,
plaster quick with spray

from the monsoon coast,
beams dripping salt.

⎯

Unable to reconcile those that are scattered
with those bound in fragile places

we turn to where alms
are collected for the poor,

identity pulled apart
on the tongs of war,

cities quivering by a slow river
which some call death.

A chance encounter
dissolves the separate things

we make out of our lives,
as if the wreckage of war

concerned us not a jot
and love were a painted concertina

played in underground passages,
in the metros of Manhattan, Paris,

Delhi, Kolkata where platform walls
bear a poet's drafts blown big,

words strummed to
bird mouths, pesky wings,

flowers with beaks of gold,
inky metamorphoses:

I have picked at them, tried to redeem them.
They cry as sinners might.

➤

Who will redeem the real,
cherish fleshly fragments:

jog of hair, splintering mole,
jolt of unlikeness,

desire that turns us lean,
each rift crammed with sweetness,

arrow roiling the eye
of whatever time there may be left,

the skin of mango and rose
wet with smoke.

━

Hear me out:
I have come to ground

in my own country,
by the Pamba's edge

in a field of golden rice
where shades gather.

One cries, I lost my leg.
Another, My arm is blown

and here is the hood
of bright hair that was my mother's mother's.

It glistens with gunfire,
please take it from me.

━

Tongues emblazon
the harpsichord of flesh,

close to a child in a wood house
where a bomb falls,

her arms and legs aflame.
A woman in a kitchen miles away

washing rice who turns
and stops to write.

Who dares to burn
with the stamp of love?

Words glimmer
then the slow

march to sentences.
Sankara speak to me.

Notes

Late, There Was an Island

In my notebook I have written down the dates of composition: "Aftermath," September 13–18, 2001; "Invisible City," October 17–November 3, 2001; "Pitfire," November 20–December 5, 2001.

AFTERMATH AND INVISIBLE CITY: These two poems saw the light of day on December 7, 2001, at the panel discussion "Artist in a Time of Crisis" at the New York Foundation for the Arts, Drawing Center, Soho. Together with "Pitfire," they were in the exhibit "Time to Consider: The Arts Respond to 9/11" (www.timetoconsider.org).

PITFIRE: "Liturgie de cristal" is Olivier Messiaen's phrase. I have taken it from his preface to part 1 of *Quatuor pour la fin de temps.* The clarinet solo is part 3 ("Abîme des oiseaux").

Listening to Lorca

After the pain and shock of September 11, it was a pleasure to read Lorca's *Poet in New York* and reattach myself to place through *some*, and I stress *some*, of his words. At times his lines startled me – "If it isn't the birds / covered with ash . . ." ("Si non los parajos / cubiertos de ceniza . . ."). I carried his poems with me as I rode on the subway, as I wandered about Central Park. One afternoon I sat in Sheep's Meadow with a friend who read out the Spanish lines to me. I felt that Lorca was speaking to me. Lorca had come as a visitor to this island and then left. I had come exactly fifty years later and stayed on. Then it happened – I started to hear Lorca's voice as I walked about the city. His voice in my ear. My response became these poems (from the 2002 catalog of *Poetry International*, Royal Festival Hall, London).

COLOR OF HOME: When Lorca was a student in New York (1929–30), he wrote a letter home enclosing a photograph that shows him walking down Morningside Drive with three friends, one of whom he describes as a "Hindu ballerina."

CASIDA OF A FLOWERING TREE: The famous line "at five in the afternoon" comes from Lorca's poem for a slain bullfighter, "Lament for Ignacio Sánchez Mejías," translated by Stephen Spender and J. L. Gili (*The Selected Poems of Federico García Lorca*, edited by Francisco García Lorca and Donald M. Allen [New York: New Directions, 1961]).

CENTRAL PARK, CAROUSEL: The last line comes from Lorca's poem "Despedida," in the translation by W. S. Merwin (*The Selected Poems of Federico García Lorca*).

Child, Stone, Sea
This poem was composed for the final night of Poetry Africa, May 4, 2002. My thanks to Chris Abani, who made me the gift of a special stone. Gugu Dlamini Park in Durban is named for a young woman with AIDS who was brutally murdered. The third stanza in the third section is a riff, with thanks, on lines by Keorapetse Willie Kgositsile, "The Present Is a Dangerous Place to Live" (*If I Could Sing* [Kwela/Snail-press, 2002]).

Raw Silk
The lines in italics in section 1 are from the loveliest of Verlaine's lyrics, "Le ciel est, par-dessus le toit" (*Sagesse*, 1880), composed while he was in prison.

Petroglyph
In an earlier version of this poem, I focused on Kant and his notions of geography. After September 11, I tore that open and worked in the thoughts of a city with its lower parts on fire. The poem as a whole was composed between April 15, 2001, and February 26, 2002. In section 4, line 8 is drawn from lines by Gwendolyn Brooks ("Second Sermon on the Warpland," in *In the Mecca* [New York: Harper and Row, 1968]). The

lines in the epigraph and in section 7 are drawn from Muriel Rukeyser's poem "Waterlily Fire": see section 1 ("The Burning") and section 2 ("The Island") in *A Muriel Rukeyser Reader*, ed. Jan Heller Levi (New York: Norton, 1994). I am grateful to David Harvey for his thoughts in "Cosmopolitanism and the Banality of Geographical Evils," *Public Culture* 12, no. 2 (2000). Without his ruminations I would know nothing of Kant's sense of geography. The painter of *Riposte* is Cecilia Edefalk.

Triptych in a Time of War

This poem was composed March 7–26, 2003, in New York City.

The poet Forugh Farrokhzad (1935–67) lived in Tehran and wrote fierce, dazzling poems. The lines in italics in section 1 are taken from her poem "O Bejewelled Land." I have drawn on the translation by Hasan Javadi and Susan Sallée in *Another Birth: Selected Poems of Forugh Farrokhzad* (Emeryville, Calif.: Albany Press, 1981). Enheduanna (circa 2300 B.C.E.) is the earliest poet known in recorded history. She lived in Mesopotamia, and her likeness is to be found on an alabaster disk preserved in the University of Pennsylvania Museum. The creator of Dove of Tanna is Frank Stella; the artwork hangs on the eastern wall of the atrium at 365 Fifth Avenue, CUNY Graduate Center.

Amrita

Inspired by the digital photomontages of Vivan Sundaram's *Retake of Amrita*, I imagine Amrita Sher-gil speaking after the Gujarat atrocities. The child Yunus I saw in a relief camp in Ahmedabad.

Searching for a Tomb over Which They Paved a Road

During the carnage in Gujarat, the tomb of the seventeenth-century Muslim poet Wali Gujarati (also known as Wali Deccani) was torn down by Hindu extremists.

Letters to Gandhi

On September 11, 2002, I was in Ahmedabad to visit the relief camps for the survivors of ethnic violence. "Letters to Gandhi" could not have come into being without two friends: Svati Joshi, who drew me to Ahmedabad; Ramu Gandhi, who still listens to me.

BENGALI MARKET: In this poem I hear the voice of Anna Akhmatova coming from the far north. The question someone asked her in "Instead of a Preface" (*Requiem*) echoed in my mind: "Can you describe this?"

Fragile Places

Sankara, the great philosopher of Advaita Vedanta, was born in Kaladi, in what is now Kerala. He believed that the phenomenal world was *maya*, zone of the unreal. The poet I refer to in the third section is Rabindranath Tagore. The two lines in italics at the close of that section are drawn from his notes on *Purabi*. Tagore comments on his own deletions: lines crossed out in the manuscript turned into doodles, the genesis of his craft as an artist. Some of these manuscript pages are displayed, blown up, on the walls of the Kolkata Underground.

Acknowledgments

My love and thanks as always to David Lelyveld and to Adam and Svati. My gratitude to friends with whom I have shared these poems: Adrienne Rich, Cecilia Edefalk, Gauri Viswanathan, Nabeel Sarwar, Ferdinando Pisani, Reginald Gibbons, Erika Duncan, Karen Malpede, Rajeshwari Sunder Rajan, Ramchandra Gandhi. At Northwestern University Press, my special thanks to Sue Betz for her care and understanding.

For the gift of time and space to compose these poems my thanks to Hunter College for a faculty fellowship; the Fulbright Foundation for a Senior Scholar Award; the Rockefeller Foundation for a residency at Villa Serbelloni, Bellagio; Fondation Ledig–Rowholt for a residency at Chateau de Lavigny; the Center for Place, Culture, Politics for a fellowship at the Graduate Center of the City University of New York.

I am grateful to the editors of the following publications where these poems first appeared:

Big City Lit: "Color of Home," "Casida of a Flowering Tree," "Central Park, Carousel"

Chandrabhaga: "Fragile Places"

Faultline: "Hard Rowing," "Lago di Como"

Harvard Review: "Ghalib's Ghost," "Triptych in a Time of War"

The Hindu (Literary Review, July 6, 2003): "Red Bird," "In Naroda Patiya," "Amrita," "Searching for a Tomb over Which They Paved a Road," "Lyric with Doves," "Slow Dancing," "Bengali Market," "Gandhi's Bicycle (My Muse Comes to Me)"

Indian Literature: "Firefly" (as "Who Am I?"), "Porta Santa," "Roman Ground"

Kenyon Review: "Raw Silk"

The Little Magazine (India): "Kabir Sings in a City of Burning Towers"

The Nation: "Ancestors"

New Coin (South Africa): "Child, Stone, Sea" (as "Kadaalinte Paatu")

Paterson Literary Review: "Green Parasol," "For a Friend Whose Father

was Killed on the Lahore Border in the 1965 War between In-
dia and Pakistan"

PEN America (special issue on literary tribes): "Blue Lotus" (as "Tribe,
Tribute, Tribulation")

Prairie Schooner: "Dialogue by a City Wall," "Opening the Shutters,"
"Field in Summer"

Rattapallax: "Bengali Market"

Social Text: "Aftermath," "Invisible City," "Pitfire," "Petroglyph"

"Rumors for an Immigrant" was commissioned by Hans–Ulrich Obrist
for Arc en Rêve, Mutations Projects on the City, in conjunction with an
exhibit of the designs of Rem Koolhaas, Jean Nouvel, Stefano Boeri,
and Sanford Kwinter (Bordeaux and Fribourg, fall 2000) and was pub-
lished in the volume *Mutations* (2000).

"Listening to Lorca" was commissioned by Ruth Borthwick for the
Royal Festival Hall, London, Poetry International 2002.

"Child, Stone, Sea" (as "Durban Song") was composed for Poetry
Africa 2002.

"Letters to Gandhi" was first printed as a chapbook by the Oxford
South Asia Forum, March 8, 2003.

About the Author

Meena Alexander was born in Allahabad, India. Her volume of poems *Illiterate Heart* won a 2002 PEN Open Book Award. Her memoir, *Fault Lines,* chosen as one of *Publishers Weekly's* Best Books of 1993, is published in a new expanded edition with a coda entitled "Book of Childhood." She lives in New York City, where she is Distinguished Professor of English at Hunter College and the Graduate Center at the City University of New York.